Contents

Riding high

Have you used a computer today? Did you browse the Internet, write some text or work on a presentation? If you did, you almost certainly used Microsoft software.

The Microsoft Corporation, founded by Bill Gates and Paul Allen in the 1970s, has changed the way we work. In those days, people relied on typewriters to write documents. You couldn't cut and paste or edit the words. To make a poster or presentation for your homework, you had to design the letters, draw the images and stick them on paper. At that time, computers were expensive and enormous – one computer took up an entire room! Only large universities and businesses had any computers. Nobody had one at home.

After the invention of the computer chip, Microsoft developed software for personal computers (PCs) so that people could have them at work and home. It made the software easy to use so that people didn't need to know anything about computer programming. Microsoft adopted a clever marketing technique, selling its operating system (the 'go between' that communicates between the software programs and the hardware) to the companies that made computers. This meant that it would make money from every computer sold. With the rise of the

▼ *As in many wealthy countries, these secondary-school students in the USA have some lessons in the computer lab.*

BIG BU$INE$$

Microsoft

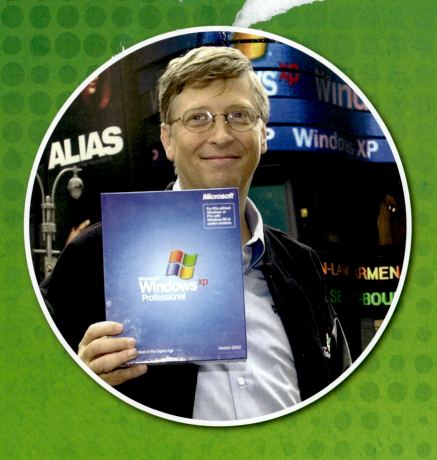

Cath Senker

Published in 2013 by Wayland

Copyright © Wayland 2013

Wayland
338 Euston Road
London NW1 3BH

Wayland Australia
Level 17/207 Kent Street
Sydney, NSW 2000

Managing editor: Debbie Foy
Designer: Emma Randall
Picture researcher: Shelley Noronha

Picture Acknowledgments: The author and publisher would like to thank the following for allowing their pictures to be reproduced in this publication: cover image: Shutterstock; 4 Jetta Productions; 6 Sipa Press/Rex Features; 7 Photoshot; 8 Bettman/Corbis; 9 Ullsteinbild/TopFoto; 10 Bettman/Corbis; 11, 12 Getty Images; 13 Reuters/Corbis; 14, 15, 16, 18 AFP/Getty Images; 17, 18 Shutterstock; 20 Photoshot/Jens Wolf; 21 Photoshot; 23 Yue Yuwei/Xinhua Press/Corbis; 24 NY Daily News via Getty Images; 25, 27 The Image Works/TopFoto; 26 Ullsteinbild/TopFoto

British Library Cataloguing in Publication Data
Senker, Cath.
Microsoft : the story behind the iconic business. -- (Big business)
1. Microsoft Corporation--Juvenile literature. 2. Computer software industry--United States--Juvenile literature.
I. Title II. Series III. Foy, Debbie.
338.7'610053'0973-dc23

ISBN: 978 0 7502 8203 1

Printed in China

10 9 8 7 6 5 4 3 2 1

Wayland is a division of Hachette Children's Books, an Hachette UK company.
www.hachette.co.uk

Business Matters

The Management of Microsoft

Main headquarters:
Redmond, Washington

Board of Directors
(9 people, 2011)

4 Operation Centres (2009)
*Licensing, Manufacturing,
Operations and Logistics* – Dublin
Manufacturing – Humacao, Puerto Rico
Licensing and Operations – Reno, Nevada
Operations and Logistics – Singapore

**Subsidiaries (companies owned
by Microsoft) around the world**
108 countries in Europe, Africa,
Asia, Australasia, America
(2011)

Employees (June 2011) 90,412
Net revenue (sales) US $69.94 billion (£44 billion)
Net income (profit) US $23.15 billion (£15 billion)

▲ *A large company needs a strong structure. This diagram shows how
Microsoft is organized.*

Internet, Microsoft brought out products such as the Internet Explorer web browser, which allowed people to access the new virtual world.

Today, Microsoft is the leading maker of software for PCs. It provides servers and software for business. The vast majority of computers worldwide use its software. Its main areas of business include the Windows operating system, including Internet Explorer; Microsoft Office software; gaming, music and video (such as Xbox); online services, such as MSN; and Skype online

communications. In 2013, the personal wealth of Microsoft's chairman, Bill Gates, totalled an incredible US $67 billion (£43 billion).

This book examines Microsoft's rise to the top of the computer software world and considers key questions. How did the company get its software on to virtually all the computers in the world? How does it continue to improve its products and expand into new areas? What are the negative sides of this business model? Finally, how does Microsoft see the future of computer software?

From small beginnings

Bill Gates and his friend Paul Allen first used computers when they were at school. They became obsessed with computer programming; even as boys they understood that computers had great potential.

A computer is made up of hardware – the parts that make up the machine itself. To make the computer work, you need software – programs that tell the computer what to do. Bill and Paul realized that computers would need software to run on them. When they were still at school, Bill and Paul set up their own company, Traf-O-Data, to sell computer programs.

In 1973, Bill went to top-class Harvard University. Two years later, while he was still studying, the company MITS brought out the first 'personal computer', the Altair 8800. But you had to build it yourself! Electronics enthusiasts ordered the kit and made up the

Altair at home. Once it was assembled, all you could do was play a game with flashing lights.

Bill and Paul understood that to make the Altair useful, it needed software. They told MITS that they could provide an easy-to-use form of a software program called BASIC that would work on the Altair. The pair succeeded in creating Altair BASIC. MITS was extremely pleased and offered Paul a job in March 1975.

Later in 1975, after Bill had finished his second year at Harvard, Bill and Paul set up Microsoft. The company provided BASIC software

Paul Allen (left) and Bill ➤
Gates, with the computers
of the day, 1981.

▲ *The staff of Microsoft in 1978, with Gates (left) and Allen (right) in the front row.*

for new versions of MITS computers. Bill left Harvard in 1977, without completing his course, to work in the business. Microsoft grew rapidly. In 1978, just three years after it was formed, Microsoft's sales topped a million dollars! The following year, the company made its first big deal in Japan, agreeing to provide software for the Nippon Electric Co (NEC). By 1980, Microsoft was earning millions of dollars a year.

> " *Over 20 years ago, even before I helped to co-found Microsoft, I saw a connected future…I called that future 'the wired world'.* "
>
> **Microsoft co-founder, Paul Allen, 1998**

Business Matters

The computer chip — In 1969 Ted Hoff, a researcher for computer corporation Intel, invented the multi-purpose computer chip. It was a tiny piece of silicon with an electronic circuit, and it allowed computers to be built far more quickly and cheaply than before. There are two types of silicon chip: the microprocessor (with instructions for computer programs) and the memory chip, which holds programs and information. The invention of the tiny computer chip provided the basis for the explosion in the personal computing business.

The launch of MS-DOS

In 1980, Microsoft pulled off an important deal. It agreed to provide the operating system for IBM's first personal computer. The following year, Bill Gates bought an operating system called 86-DOS from another computing company. Based on 86-DOS, Microsoft created its own OS called the Microsoft Disk Operating System – MS-DOS.

After this, most PC producers bought MS-DOS as their OS, bringing huge sales for Microsoft. By 1981, Bill Gates and Paul Allen had become celebrities in the computing world.

At this time, computer software experts were continually arriving at the doors of Microsoft to offer their ideas. One was Charles Simonyi from Hungary. At his previous company, he had developed What You See Is What You Get (WYSIWYG) word processing. What you saw on the screen looked the same when you printed it out. In 1981, Gates gave him a job. Others flocked to Microsoft, eager for a post in this exciting new industry. In November 1981, the company took on its 100th employee and then moved to bigger offices.

Conditions at Microsoft were good. Soft drinks were provided free of charge, the offices were

▼ *An IBM computer in use in 1987, running Microsoft's MS-DOS.*

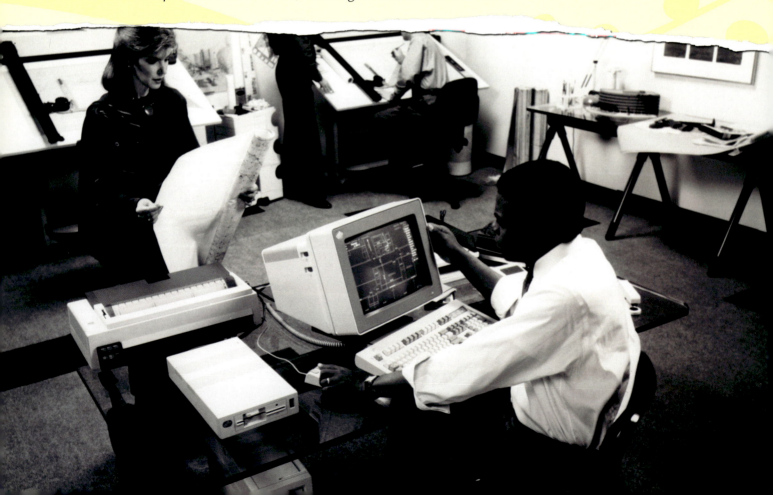

roomy and comfortable, and employees could communicate via email. This was a novelty in the 1980s! Yet working at Microsoft was tough – employees were often required to work 14-hour days, seven days a week. Although the workers were keen and enthusiastic, this tough working life could prove bad for their health.

Brains Behind The Brand

Paul Allen, co-founder of Microsoft
Born in Seattle, Washington, in 1953, Paul Allen attended Lakeside School, the same private school as Bill Gates. The boys shared a great enthusiasm for computers. Paul went on to Washington State University in 1973. He worked with Bill to adapt BASIC, a programming language for large computers, to work on personal computers. Paul dropped out of college after two years and took a job as a computer programmer. In 1976, after founding Microsoft, he went to work for the company full-time. In 1980, he and Bill made the crucial deal to provide IBM with MS-DOS software. This enabled Microsoft to become the leading company in the PC boom of the 1980s.

Business Matters

Commission — In business, commission is an amount of money that is paid to a person or company for selling goods. When IBM launched its PC in August 1981, it had MS-DOS as the operating system. IBM had agreed that Microsoft would receive commission for every PC sold. But Microsoft could also sell its operating system to other computer manufacturers. This was a smart business move.

◄ *Charles Simonyi created Bravo, the first WYSIWYG text editor, in the 1970s.*

Opening Windows, 1985

In the early 1980s, most computers came with the MS-DOS operating system. Computer users needed to know some programming terms. They had to type 'C' and various commands to tell their computer what to do.

In 1984, Apple produced the first computer with a Graphical User Interface (GUI). Instead of using commands, the desktop had icons (little images) for the programs. You could point and click on them with a mouse. To delete a file, you dragged and dropped it in the trash can.

In November 1985, Microsoft introduced Windows 1.0, with its own GUI – a major breakthrough for PC users. Now, users could point and click on various screens, or 'windows' to instruct the computer. There were drop-down menus with various options. You could open more than one document at the same time and switch between different programs without having to close each one down first.

However, Windows 1.0 had some problems. You could not overlap your documents on the screen. Each program used up so much memory that the computer often crashed. The product wasn't quite ready for use, and Microsoft was accused of bringing out Windows too soon. The company's software developers continued to work on it to fix the bugs (errors).

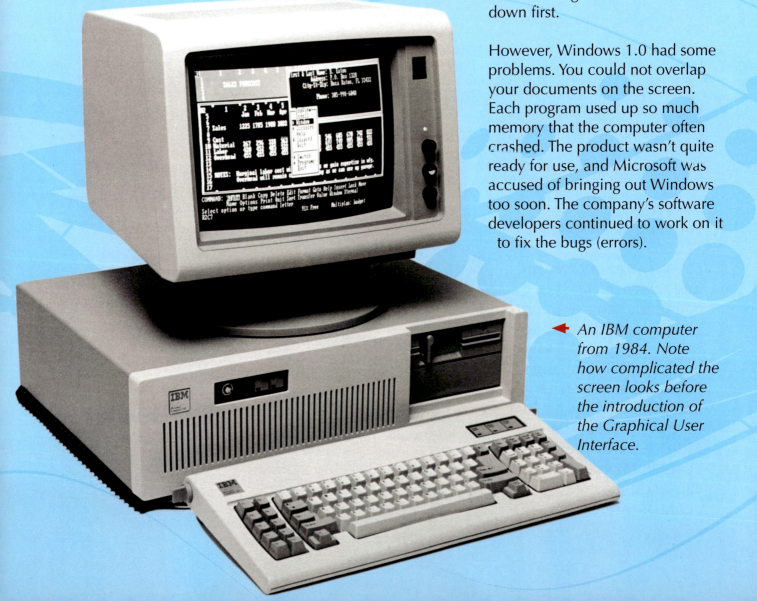

An IBM computer from 1984. Note how complicated the screen looks before the introduction of the Graphical User Interface.

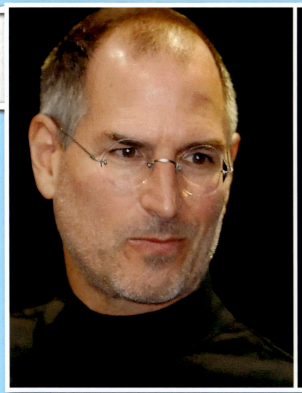 

▲ *Steve Jobs (left) and Bill Gates in 2007, during a period when Apple and Microsoft were co-operating.*

Business Matters

Competition and cooperation — Different companies in the same business may sometimes act as competitors but at other times cooperate to help each other. This happened with Microsoft and Apple.

Steve Jobs and Steve Wozniak developed the first Apple computer in 1976. In 1982, Microsoft signed a contract with Apple to develop software for its computer, now known as the Apple Macintosh, or Mac. Bill asked his researchers to develop a Graphical User interface for the Mac that could also be used on IBM PCs. This way, Microsoft could produce software for both types of computer, which made good business sense. After all, IBM was still the biggest computer hardware company, and it used Microsoft software.

Relations between Microsoft and Apple turned sour though. In 1987, Windows 2.0 was launched. Apple claimed that the idea for Windows had been stolen from Apple's software and took Microsoft to court. In a second court case, it accused Microsoft of illegally copying its rectangular boxes with commands. Yet in 1992, both the claims were overturned.

In 1997, the two companies returned to cooperation. Under a new agreement, Microsoft would produce Microsoft Office and Internet Explorer for the Mac. Microsoft and Apple would share the patent and licensing agreements — the ownership of the products and the income from selling them.

'A computer on every desk'

Despite initial problems with Windows, Microsoft dominated the software market in the mid-1980s. In 1986, it became a public company. Instead of being owned purely by the people who had set it up, the company could sell shares to the public. Bill Gates became a billionaire overnight because he owned most of the shares. In the same year, the rapidly expanding company, now employing 1,200 workers, moved to new headquarters in Redmond, Washington.

▲ *Bill Gates at the Redmond headquarters in 1986.*

Improved versions of Windows continued to appear. In 1987, Windows 2.0 came out, with desktop icons and more memory. You could overlap windows and use keyboard shortcuts (touching a key or two to choose an action rather than using the mouse). The software as well as the operating system was progressing too. Most significant was the introduction of Microsoft Office in 1989, with its group of programs including Microsoft Word and Microsoft Excel – some of the most popular software programs in the world today.

Launched in 1990, the new, faster Windows 3.0 proved extremely popular. By 1993, one million copies were sold every month. Worldwide, almost 90 per cent of all PCs ran on Windows. Microsoft seemed unstoppable. It was the largest computer industry in world.

Despite the growth of the industry, in the early 1990s, many people – even in wealthy countries – still did not know how to use a computer. Also, although large numbers used computers at work, they did not have a PC at home.

In 1994, Microsoft launched a $100-million (£63 million) advertising campaign to try to appeal to ordinary people who didn't use computers yet. The slogan was 'Where do you want to go today?' Bill Gates knew that the computer revolution still had a long way to go before there was 'a computer on every desk'.

This graph shows the remarkably rapid rise of Microsoft's sales during its first decade.

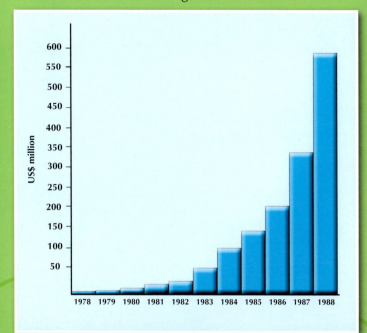

US$ million

Brains Behind The Brand

Jeff Raikes, the 'Godfather of Office'

Jeff Raikes went to work for Apple in 1980 but after 15 months, Steve Ballmer recruited him to Microsoft. He was promoted to Director of Applications Marketing in 1984. Jeff was responsible for developing the design of the Microsoft Office suite of applications, creating a multi-million-dollar product that most people have on their computers. For his work, Jeff became known as the 'Godfather of Office'.

Jeff Raikes in 2002, when he was group vice-president of Productivity and Business Services at Microsoft.

> " A computer on every desk and in every home, running Microsoft software. "
>
> **Microsoft slogan since the late 1980s**

Bill Gates: the man behind Microsoft

Born in Seattle, USA in 1955, William Henry Gates excelled at maths and science at school. He was fascinated by the new world of computers. At Lakeside School, he and his friends Paul Allen, Rick Weiland and Kent Evans formed the Lakeside Programmers Club. The school had no computers but the teachers rented them for the students.

The boys computerized the school timetable and the payroll (list of workers and their wages) for a local business. In 1972, Bill and Paul founded their own company, Traf-O-Data, which developed a traffic-counting system for local governments. At the time, Bill said to Paul about computers: 'Don't you think that someday everybody will have one of these things?' He also stated 'I'm going to make a million dollars by the time I'm 20.' Bill and Paul continued to spend as much time as possible working on software.

In 1973, Bill went to Harvard University but he dropped out to focus on building Microsoft. A natural risk taker, he later put all of Microsoft's resources into developing Windows. Fortunately, the gamble paid off both times. In 1983, Bill was left to head the company alone after Paul developed cancer and stepped down from Microsoft.

Bill married Melinda French in 1994, and their daughter Jennifer Katharine was born in 1996. In 1995, Bill published his story, *The Road Ahead*, which became a worldwide bestseller. People were fascinated with the man and his enormous fortune.

In 2008, Bill left his role as chief software architect although he continued as chairman. He committed his time to the Bill and Melinda Gates Foundation, a

◄ *Bill Gates is known worldwide; here he appears on the front cover of a Vietnamese magazine, in 2006.*

🔺 *Bill Gates at a press conference with Club Barcelona in 2011 to announce a partnership to work towards ending the disease polio.*

global health and development charity he and his wife had formed in 2000. The foundation aims to reduce poverty and improve health care and education by using science and technology – for example, by supplying vaccines to prevent childhood diseases. In this way, Bill believed he could give back to society some of the huge benefits he had gained.

> " I think it's fair to say that personal computers have become the most empowering tool we've ever created. They're tools of communication, they're tools of creativity, and they can be shaped by their user. "
>
> **Bill Gates, 1972**

Brains Behind The Brand

Bill Gates, CEO

Bill Gates was Chief Executive Officer (CEO) of Microsoft until 2000. He had the vision of PCs for all, and pushed his software developers to produce a GUI so that users would need no computing knowledge to operate a computer. When the Internet age arrived in the 1990s, Microsoft produced the Internet Explorer web browser, which became one of the most popular ways of accessing the Internet. Under Bill's leadership, Windows became the most popular OS worldwide, used by nine-tenths of all computers. Bill Gates is seen as one of the world's most important figures in the development of the computer industry.

The Internet takes off

Nowadays, we take the Internet for granted. But until the 1990s, few people had access to it. Between 1994 and 1999, the number of users soared from 3 million to more than 200 million. Yet Microsoft remained focused on PC software. It was a little slow to work out how to make money from the Internet.

In 1995, Microsoft introduced Windows 1995, its most ambitious package yet. This OS allowed users to work on several software programs at the same time. Windows 1995 made it simple to go online. It had built-in dial-up networking (in those days, you had to dial up the Internet, rather like making a phone call). It had Plug and Play: new hardware, such as a video card, worked as soon as it was connected. Windows 95 was fully integrated with the MS-DOS operating system, which made it work well. Microsoft also led the field with its word-processing and spreadsheet software – Microsoft Word and Excel.

Microsoft blitzed the marketing of Windows 95, announcing in its press release, 'It's here.' The corporation held parties and big media events, and broadcast TV adverts. Within just four days, 1 million copies of Windows 95 were sold in North America alone! Windows 95 sales greatly boosted Microsoft's profits for the year.

◄ *Internet users at an Internet cafe in Beijing, China.*

Business Matters

Software for business — In the 1990s, Microsoft put efforts into developing software for businesses and large organizations. In 1993, it released Windows NT, the first of its server and business operating systems. A server is a computer that runs services for the computers on its network. For example, a file server keeps files and allows all the users on the network to access them. To work with Windows NT, the company also developed Microsoft SQL Server for creating and managing databases. Another important development was Microsoft Outlook, first released as part of Microsoft Office 1997. Including an email program, contacts, calendar, note taking and a journal, it was the perfect tool for people to organize their work. Microsoft also produced software especially for business desktop and laptop computers, such as Windows 2000 Professional.

Not content with dominating the software market, Microsoft wanted to compete for online services. In 1994, rival corporation Netscape Communications had introduced the web browser Netscape Navigator. Now Microsoft raced to catch up. In 1995 Bill Gates made it clear that the Internet had become a priority. That year MSN was launched to provide online services – within two years, MSN included online news and Hotmail web-based email. Microsoft also brought out the first version of Internet Explorer in 1995. It was bundled (included) for free with the Windows OS. Most PC owners now used a Microsoft product to browse the web.

The PCs of office workers are often linked to a network so they can all access company information and software.

New Windows to the world

By 2000, computers were common at home as well as in workplaces. Even people with no computer at home or work could get online at an Internet café or their local library. Now people were using their PC for leisure and entertainment as well as for work. Microsoft designed new versions of Windows for home as well as business use.

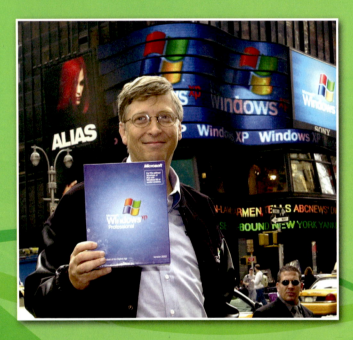

Bill Gates launches Windows XP in 2001.

This Windows edition was targeted at the home entertainment market.

As well as improving its software, Microsoft grew increasingly concerned about software piracy – when people illegally copy and share software instead of buying it. Windows XP, launched in 2001 in both Home and Professional versions, was the first OS that the user had to activate. This meant no one else could use it. The next major OS, Windows Vista (introduced in 2006), focused on security, making it hard for criminals to hack into people's computers and damage them with computer viruses or steal their personal data. But Vista had problems; it required an extremely fast computer with large amounts of memory to work properly. Therefore, large numbers of business and home users stuck with XP.

By 2009, computer use had shifted again. More people were buying laptops than desktop PCs. Netbooks – which were smaller, lighter and cheaper than regular laptops – became popular too. People used their computer on the go, accessing the web in wireless hotspots that became available in places such as cafés, hotels and railway stations. To make it easier to use a computer on the move, the next OS, Windows 7 (launched 2009), included Windows Touch. With a touch screen, you could use your fingers to open files, browse the web, flip through photos and access music and video. In October 2012, Windows 8 was launched, followed by the updated Windows 8.1 in late 2013.

▼ *By 2012, Windows 7 was the most popular OS. Note the small percentage of users of non-Microsoft operating systems.*

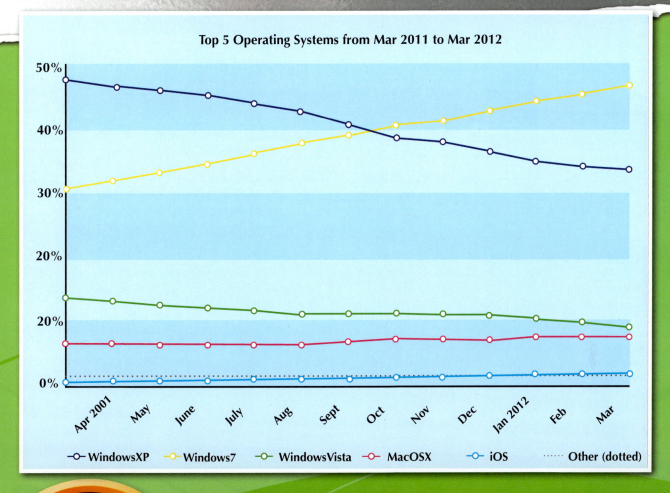

Top 5 Operating Systems from Mar 2011 to Mar 2012

—○— WindowsXP   —○— Windows7   —○— WindowsVista   —○— MacOSX   —○— iOS   ······ Other (dotted)

Business Matters

Market dominance — Critics of Microsoft accuse the corporation of being too dominant in the market. They argue that it makes vast profits because of the high cost of its products. It's not possible to buy cheaper versions of Microsoft software. Microsoft's licensing policy prevents sharing — you cannot copy its software on to another computer without paying. Others complain because they prefer to use a free open-source OS (an OS that anyone can use and improve), such as Linux. But PCs come with Windows installed, and buyers have no choice in the matter.

Legal action has been taken against Microsoft's dominance. For example, in 2004, the European Union (EU) fined the company US $611 million (£385 million) for acting like a monopoly — controlling the entire market for software because there is no other similar product. The EU fined Microsoft more than double this amount in 2008 for illegally including multimedia software with Windows and not allowing competitors to include their software.

Entering the games world: Xbox

Are you into computer games? Do you use a Sony PlayStation, a Nintendo or an Xbox console? Microsoft entered the multi-million-dollar games console market in 2001 with the Xbox.

The first Xbox included the Rallisport Challenge racing game and combat game Halo, among others. It had an online service, so users could compete with others over the Internet. However, the Xbox was not successful, partly because the console had an expensive hard drive. The company made losses totalling US$3.7 billion.

In 2005, Microsoft brought out the Xbox 360, which was much cheaper to make. It invested in a huge global marketing campaign with the slogan 'Live your Moment'. Microsoft aimed to turn Xbox into a popular entertainment platform for families and friends to play regularly, not just committed gamers. The idea was to encourage people to buy the console. Then they would be locked into buying new games for it; most of the profits came from games sales. But Microsoft still found its profits were low. In 2009, it reduced the price of the Xbox 360 Elite from $399 to $299 in the USA. This move encouraged sales.

▼ *Business visitors check out the Xbox 360 stand at a games convention in 2006.*

Steve Ballmer in 2009. In 2012 he introduced Windows tablet computers and the first of a new generation of Windows Phones.

Microsoft's next strategy was to buy Kinect in 2010 to compete with the Nintendo Wii. With Kinect, you no longer needed a controller or remote. You could use your whole body to play games – jumping, kicking or dancing as necessary. Using your voice, you could access movies, music and TV or play games with people around the world. This technology allowed Xbox to successfully compete with Sony PlayStation. By 2012, the Xbox 360 was the best-selling games console, overtaking the Sony PlayStation and Nintendo Wii. Microsoft had cracked the games console market.

Brains Behind The Brand

Steve Ballmer, CEO

Bill Gates appointed Steve Ballmer, a friend from Harvard University, as business manager in 1980. Steve took over all the administration of the company: the finances, legal affairs and human resources work (managing the staff). He rose to become CEO in 2000. It was Ballmer who handled the challenge of entering the games market, introducing the Xbox in 2001.

In 2008, when Gates left, Ballmer took over the day-to-day running of the company. He developed Bing, a Microsoft search engine to compete with Google, and in 2011 he acquired Skype – the largest buy-out in Microsoft's history. Always with an eye on the future, he became enthusiastic about developing cloud computing.

> " I test the games to ensure that they are ready for release. I love my job. I get to be a big kid. I get to do what I like doing as a job and get to do it well. It's fantastic fun. "
>
> **Sally Reynolds, professional games tester for Xbox 360 games**

Into the clouds

By 2010, more and more people were going online using their mobiles or tablet computers such as iPads. They wanted to access their software and files wherever they were, without having to store them on the device. So software developers went into the 'clouds'.

Microsoft is a major developer of cloud computing, allowing people to connect wirelessly to all their resources, wherever they are. In cloud computing, computer programs are delivered as a service rather than a physical product. People working for a company can share resources, software and information over a network on the Internet. They can access them from computers, laptops, tablet computers or mobiles. The software and data are stored on

servers. You may be using cloud computing yourself. If you have a web-based email account, such as Hotmail or Yahoo, you are using cloud computing. The software and emails are not on your computer or phone – they are on the email provider's computer cloud.

Cloud computing has several benefits. Current licensing rules mean that each individual has to buy the software they need for their computer.

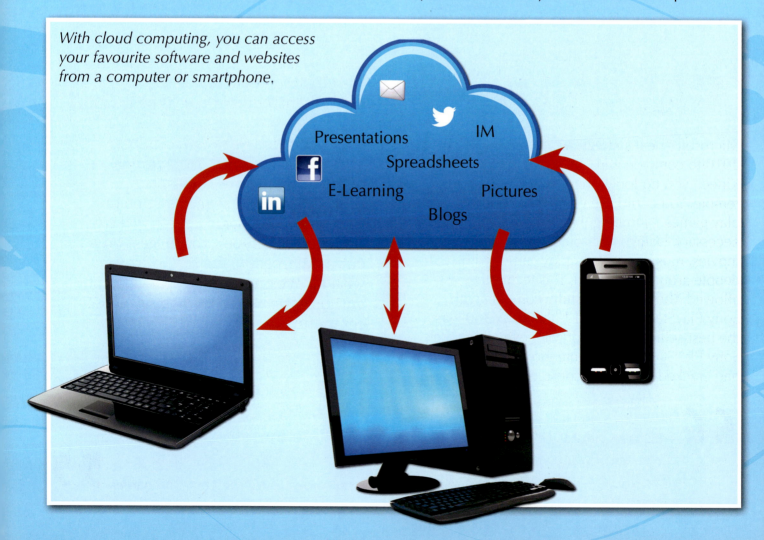

With cloud computing, you can access your favourite software and websites from a computer or smartphone.

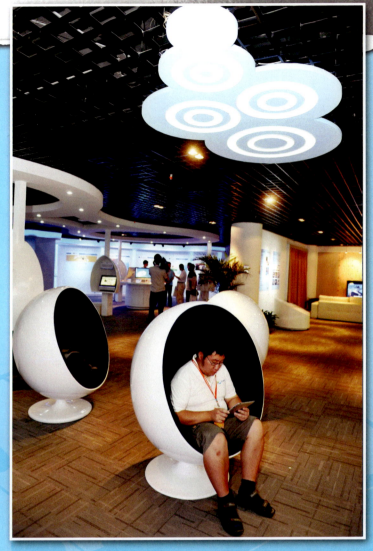

At the Cloud Centre in Tianjin, north China, an information service is provided using cloud computing.

> " One of my key team members lives and works in the L.A. [Los Angeles] area. With Microsoft Lync [communications software], she is able to stay connected through online meetings, instant messaging and email, all of which are accessible via her PC or Windows Phone. Her location doesn't hinder her productivity [productive working]. . . . Another person on my team has to leave the office early each day to pick-up her son from daycare. Remote [distance] working technologies make it easy for her to have a flexible schedule and enable her to get back online from home to wrap-up any remaining tasks from the day if needed. "
>
> **Chan Jones, Director of Cloud Services at Microsoft, Redmond, Washington**

With cloud computing, a group of people on a network share resources, so this brings down the cost. Cloud computing can help people to work from home, which is especially useful for parents with young children or those who want to reduce travelling to work.

So how will cloud computing affect you? It has great possibilities in education. Rather than buying computers and paying for software licensing, schools can take advantage of using email, spreadsheets, word processing, presentations and media editing on cloud computing. You and your classmates and teachers could all have a handheld device linked to the school network.

Yet Microsoft is not alone in this market. Google, the powerful Internet search-engine company, also develops web-based apps for businesses in competition with Microsoft. Google is probably the only company large enough to challenge the software giant.

Microsoft in the community

Microsoft donates some of its vast profits to help ordinary people of all ages and backgrounds, using its resources to provide community groups with ICT products and training. It also encourages Microsoft employees to volunteer in their communities.

For instance, in Dubai in the United Arab Emirates, few ICT workers are women. In partnership with local organizations, Microsoft organized the Dubai DigiGirlz Day to encourage more girls to study ICT in the hope that they would start to consider it as a possible career. On the day, the girls took a test with 30 questions on essential computing skills.

"The event has inspired me to explore a career in computers. There are students who don't use computers, and they should be encouraged to do so."

Afra Al Majid, 13, student at Al Alfia School for Girls, who has benefited from the Dubai DigiGirlz Day

▼ *Bill Gates talks to school students about using laptops as a learning tool.*

▲ *The children of 'scavenger' families in Bekasi, Indonesia, learn to use a computer in a free class located 50 metres from the dump's entrance.*

Only a few passed the test, indicating their general lack of knowledge about the technology. During the day, the girls took part in a workshop using Microsoft products such as Movie Maker, blogging and Microsoft Research AutoCollage (which helps you to make collages from your images). They worked with Microsoft volunteers to create an artistic piece. The aim was to show the girls that ICT is for everyone, not just for geeks!

In many countries, children do not have access to computers at all. In 2012, Microsoft announced that it was helping to fund a project to bring ICT to schools in six sub-Saharan African countries, including Kenya, Tanzania and Uganda, by establishing 80 digital hubs (centres) connected to the Internet. Where schools are not linked to the electricity grid, they will be supported by solar power. The teachers will be trained to integrate

ICT in their lessons. After school hours, people in the community will be able to use the digital hubs for training and as Internet cafés.

Microsoft also offers technological assistance in emergencies. For example, after a massive earthquake and tsunami hit Sendai in Japan in 2011, communications were wiped out in the disaster area. Microsoft provided a cloud-based disaster response communications portal (link to the Internet), based on Windows Azure, a cloud computing service. This allowed governments and aid organizations to communicate among themselves and with the Japanese people. Microsoft also used all its online properties, such as search engine Bing, MSN online services and the Microsoft.com website to provide information and weblinks to make it easy for people to donate money.

Microsoft's vision

How does Microsoft see information technology developing over the next five to ten years? Within a decade, many people will have a small electronic notebook to organize their home, work and social life.

Imagine you've time-travelled to 2020. It's the weekend and you need to do your homework. You can access all the details and the software you need on your notebook through cloud computing. Your teacher has provided a list of links to useful resources. Using speech and touch, you quickly design a presentation. Then a problem comes up. Your older brother would know the answer but he's abroad, so you call him on the video phone. (Voice calls were added to Microsoft Office after it bought Skype in 2011.) He takes over your notebook remotely to show you some helpful information. Using gestures, as with the Wii or Xbox, you tweak your work until you're happy with it.

Now you're hungry. You decide to make a new recipe. The notebook guides you through the process, with photos, videos and spoken instructions. There's no need to worry about

▼ *Cloud computing conference at the Microsoft exhibition stand in Hanover, Germany, 2011.*

burning the food; the computer on the oven switches off once the meal is perfectly cooked.

While you're waiting for your meal, you plan a trip to the water park with your friends. Your notebook provides the details of the bus journey, including the exact departure time. You can see how many people are at the water park so you can choose a quiet time. When your group arrives, you're too excited to contact your mum, but luckily your notebook tells her you've arrived safely. The staff are expecting you; your friend's mum has already paid for you, and the changing room is ready.

This vision will prove inaccurate because technology will advance in ways that we cannot imagine now. Yet we can be fairly certain that the Microsoft Corporation will continue to attract some of the best and brightest minds in computing to develop the way forward. Whether we're using a laptop, tablet, mobile or a new platform yet to be invented, we will probably continue to use Microsoft software for a long time to come.

> " We always overestimate the change that will occur in the next two years and underestimate the change that will occur in the next ten. Don't let yourself be lulled into inaction. "
>
> **From The Road Ahead, 1995**
> **Bill Gates**

▼ *A nurse in Accra, Ghana counsels patients in remote villages via mobile phone.*

To create a new product, it is helpful to put together a product development brief like the one below. This is a sample brief for Microsoft Simple Office.

The SWOT analysis on the page opposite can help you to think about the strengths and weaknesses of your products, and the opportunities and threats presented. This helps you to see how practical your idea is before you think of investing in it.

Product Development Brief

Name of product: Microsoft Simple Office

Design of logo:

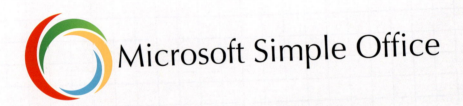

The product explained (use 25 words or less): An easy version of Microsoft Office for children, people with literacy problems (difficulty reading and writing) and those not used to computers.

Target age of consumers: All ages.

What does the product do? It has all the Microsoft Office programs, including Word, Excel, OneNote and Powerpoint, but in simple versions.

Are there any similar products available? None that I know of.

What makes your product different? The product is specially designed in simple English.

Name of Microsoft product you are assessing . . . Microsoft Simple Office. The information below will help you assess the venture. By addressing all four areas, you can make your product stronger and more likely to be a success.

Questions to consider	Strengths
Does your application do something unique?	*Yes. No other software is so simple to use.*
Is there anything innovative about it?	*Microsoft developed Microsoft Bob, a graphical user interface for novices, in 1995. It failed because of hardware problems.*
What are its USPs? (unique selling points)	*Designed to be easy to read and follow. If you find the standard version of Office hard to use you will welcome this application.*

	Weaknesses
Why wouldn't people use this application?	*If they already have Microsoft Office, they may not wish to buy another suite (set) of programs.*
Is it as good or better than other applications already available?	*The programs need to be easy to use so there will be fewer features than the standard Office suite offers.*
Do you have a technical support team in place?	*Support staff would be trained to deal with the particular needs of users, some of whom may be elderly or have learning disabilities.*

	Opportunities
Will new markets emerge for this application?	*The product may prove popular with learners of English worldwide.*
Could it be sold globally?	*Yes. It can be translated into other languages.*

	Threats
Is the market for applications shrinking?	*Most people use Microsoft Office so there may not be a big enough market for this version.*
Are any of the weaknesses so bad that they might affect the success of the venture in the long term?	*In the medium term, the weaknesses are not great but technology is moving so fast that it is impossible to make long-term predictions.*

Do you have what it takes to work at Microsoft? Try this quiz!

Do you have what it takes to work in a fast-moving global software engineering environment? Find out here!

1. Which job environment would you prefer?
a) I'd like to work outdoors in an active job.
b) I'd like to be partly desk based but maybe travel too.
c) I'd be happy in front of a computer all day long.

2. What's your attitude to computers?
a) They're useful for doing homework, watching TV and chatting to friends but I only use the most basic programs.
b) I'm quite confident about using different software programs.
c) I've tried out every program on the school computers and enjoy looking for the weak points.

3. How do you tackle your ICT homework?
a) I do as little as possible as quickly as possible.
b) I make sure I've answered all parts of the question.
c) I check out the latest information on websites and in technology magazines to make sure my project is the best.

4. Do you like computer games?
a) No, I never play them.
b) Yes, I'm always on the look-out for the newest game.
c) Yes, I love them. I have many ideas for games as well as lots of suggestions for improving the ones I play.

5. What do you do if there's a problem with the computer?
a) Ask my mum or dad to sort it out.
b) Try the obvious things, such as turning if off and on again.
c) Go through all the Help menus and search on the Internet for the solution. I love working things out for myself.

6. Do you enjoy art and design?
a) No, it's not my kind of thing.
b) I like well-designed websites and games – it makes using them more fun.
c) I have a passion for art and design and have already designed my own website.

7. What are your favourite pastimes?
a) I love sport and going out with my friends.
b) Playing video games and watching TV.
c) Making up computer games and computer programming – I'm already an expert.

Results

Mostly As: You don't seem particularly suited to a career in software at the moment. See if you can improve your keyboard skills and work on your maths and problem-solving skills.

Mostly Bs: You clearly have an interest in software. Try to improve your knowledge of software programs and develop your maths and problem-solving skills.

Mostly Cs: You're just the kind of person Microsoft will be looking for! Keep up the good work but make sure that you focus on the rest of your education as well.

Glossary

app Short for 'application', a computer program that allows people to do a particular activity, for example, send emails.

Chief Executive Officer The person at the top of a business company.

chief software architect The person in charge of developing software systems.

cloud computing A way of using computers in which data and software programs are mostly stored on a computer; the user accesses them over the Internet.

command An instruction to a computer.

computer chip An electronic circuit that forms the basis of many electronic devices.

database A set of data on a computer that can be looked at and used in various ways.

flash drive A memory device for storing data.

Graphical User Interface (GUI) A way of giving instructions to a computer using things on the screen, such as menus and symbols.

hardware The physical parts of a computer, including the machinery and electronic parts.

ICT Information and communications technology – including computers, the Internet, video and audio technology.

licensing To give someone permission to own or use something, for example, computer software.

logistics The practical organization needed to make a complicated plan successful.

multimedia Using sound, pictures and video as well as text.

network A number of computers or other devices, such as printers, that are linked together so that information and equipment can be shared.

operating system The 'go between' that communicates between the software programs and the hardware to make your computer work.

program and programming A set of instructions in code that control the operation of a computer. A programmer writes programs.

search engine A computer program that searches the Internet for information, usually by looking for documents that contain a particular words or group of words.

server A computer that supplies information to many computers connected in a network.

share A company is divided into many equal units called shares. People can buy shares to own part of the company and receive a part of the profits.

software The programs that run a computer.

spreadsheet A program used for accounts, for example, to keep a record of how much money you earn and how much you spend.

subsidiaries Companies that are controlled by another company because the other company owns the majority of the shares in it.

tablet computer A small computer contained in a flat screen. You use a stylus, digital pen or your fingertip to operate it.

web browser A program that lets you look at documents on the Internet, for example, Google.

wireless Communications that use radio waves instead of plugging in a wire, for example, computer networks.

wireless hotspot A place in a public area, such as a station or café, where you can connect to the Internet without plugging in a wire.

Index